WORLD EXPLORERS

JACQUES CARTIER

Kristin Petrie

Checkerboard Library

An Imprint of Abdo Publishing
abdobooks.com

ABDOBOOKS.COM

Published by Abdo Publishing, a division of ABDO, PO Box 398166, Minneapolis, Minnesota 55439. Copyright © 2022 by Abdo Consulting Group, Inc. International copyrights reserved in all countries. No part of this book may be reproduced in any form without written permission from the publisher. Checkerboard Library™ is a trademark and logo of Abdo Publishing.

Printed in the United States of America, North Mankato, Minnesota
102021
012022

Design and Production: Tamara JM Peterson, Mighty Media, Inc.
Editor: Liz Salzmann
Cover Photograph: Wikimedia Commons
Interior Photographs: Alamy Photo, p. 21; Alejandro Lafuente Lopez/Shutterstock Images, p. 25 (left); Anónimo/Wikimedia Commons, pp. 22–23, 29 (top); Daniel Ouellette/Shutterstock Images, p. 27; Eric L Tollstam/Shutterstock, p. 17; Jean Clouet/Wikimedia Commons, pp. 15, 28 (top); kirill_makarov/Shutterstock Images, p. 25 (right); Leonard Zhukovsky/Shutterstock Images, p. 7; Library of Congress, p. 14; Ludovic Chambaud/Shutterstock Images, p. 9; MicroOne/Shutterstock Images, pp. 12–13; Pascal Guay/Shutterstock Images, p. 19; Pierre Jean Durieu/Shutterstock Images, p. 29 (bottom); Théophile Hamel/Wikimedia Commons, pp. 5, 28 (bottom); World History Archive/Alamy Photo, p. 11
Design Elements: Joseph Moxon/Flickr (map), Oleg Iatsun/Shutterstock Images (compass rose)

Library of Congress Control Number: 2021942972

Publisher's Cataloging-in-Publication Data
Names: Petrie, Kristin, author.
Title: Jacques Cartier / by Kristin Petrie
Description: Minneapolis, Minnesota : Abdo Publishing, 2022 | Series: World explorers | Includes online resources and index.
Identifiers: ISBN 9781532197260 (lib. bdg.) | ISBN 9781098219390 (ebook)
Subjects: LCSH: Cartier, Jacques, 1491-1557--Juvenile literature. | Discovery and exploration--Juvenile literature. | Exploring expeditions--Juvenile literature. | Explorers--Biography--Juvenile literature.
Classification: DDC 970.01--dc23

CONTENTS

JACQUES CARTIER 4

BEFORE CANADA 6

FIRST VOYAGE 8

SECOND VOYAGE 14

THIRD VOYAGE 20

CARTIER'S LEGACY 26

TIMELINE 28

GLOSSARY 30

SAYING IT 31

ONLINE RESOURCES 31

INDEX 32

JACQUES CARTIER

The 1400s and 1500s were a time of exploration. Explorers from Europe were taking to the water. What lay across the Atlantic Ocean? What riches were to be found? These were the questions they wanted to answer.

Jacques Cartier was one of these explorers. In the 1500s, this Frenchman searched for a northern sea route to China. Explorers called this fabled route the **Northwest Passage**. On his search, Cartier ended up in Canada near the St. Lawrence River.

Cartier became the first European to sail up the St. Lawrence. He is known for mapping the river and the area around it. He also attempted to establish a settlement there. Cartier's explorations were the basis for France's claim to this land.

Jacques Cartier

BEFORE CANADA

Jacques Cartier was born in 1491 in Saint-Malo, France. Not much is known of Jacques's early life. There is no record of his schooling. Some experts believe, however, that he studied navigation in the city of Dieppe. This was a French center for navigators.

Some scholars believe Jacques made several trips across the Atlantic Ocean as a young man. He may have worked on a fishing **fleet** that sailed near the Grand Banks of Newfoundland. He may also have visited Brazil.

In 1520, Jacques married Catherine des Granches. Four years later, it is believed he may have sailed with Italian navigator Giovanni da Verrazano to the North American coast. Verrazano sailed along the coast from North Carolina to Newfoundland. His work contributed greatly to European knowledge of the east coast of North America.

There is a statue of Giovanni da Verrazano in Battery Park in New York City.

7

FIRST VOYAGE

In 1534, King Francis I of France hired Cartier to explore the possibility of a passage to Asia. He encouraged Cartier to claim land for France and discover countries with gold and other valuables.

Cartier's first voyage began on April 20, 1534. He sailed from Saint-Malo with two ships and a crew of 61 men. It took just 20 days to reach Cape Bonavista, Newfoundland. Cartier sailed north around the tip of Newfoundland and south between Newfoundland and Labrador. Cartier named this waterway the Strait of Belle Isle. He then discovered that the strait led to a gulf.

Cartier crossed the gulf to Prince Edward Island and the Magdalen Islands. He continued past them and reached Gaspé **Peninsula**. He claimed the peninsula for France. While exploring this region, Cartier met the area's **indigenous** people, the Mi'kmaq. The Mi'kmaq were friendly and eager to trade. The French and Mi'kmaq began exchanging iron knives and hatchets for furs.

Saint-Malo is a walled city on the coast of France. In the 1500s, many explorers left from and returned to its busy port.

The French were also friendly with the Iroquois, another Native American nation from the region. The Iroquois told Cartier of jewels, metals, and wealthy kingdoms farther to the northwest.

Cartier visited with Iroquois chief Donnacona. Cartier convinced Donnacona to allow his two sons to journey to France. The boys would learn French and become **interpreters** for Cartier. However, some experts believe that Cartier kidnapped the boys.

On July 25, Cartier and his crew returned to their ships and sailed farther north. They explored the island of Anticosti. At the western end of Anticosti Island, Cartier noted the mouth of a large river. However, Cartier's crew said strong winds made sailing on the river too dangerous. Cartier listened to them and agreed to return to France. On September 5, 1534, the ships reached Saint-Malo. The entire voyage had lasted 15 weeks.

WOULD YOU?

Would you turn back if you discovered a river that you thought could take you to Asia? How do you think the crew convinced Cartier to head home?

Cartier and his crew placed a large cross on the Gaspé Peninsula when they claimed it for France.

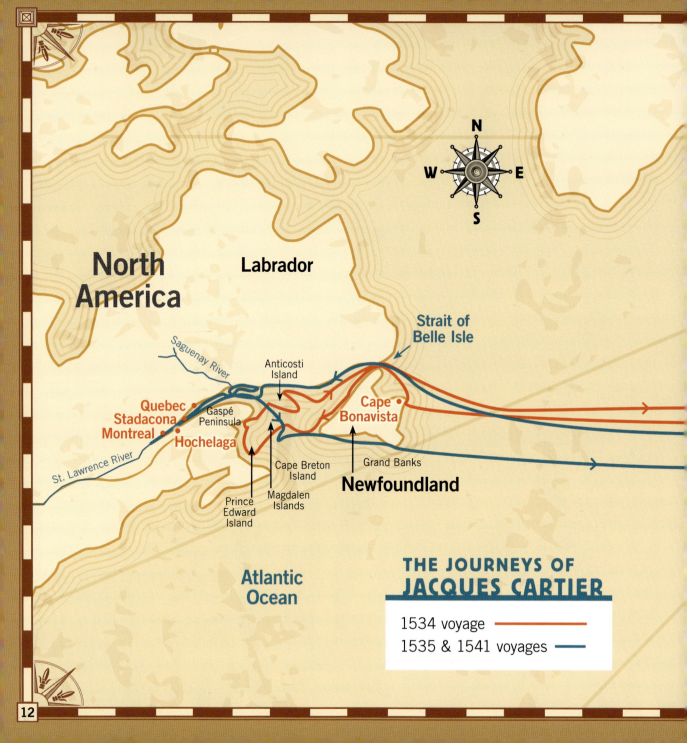

SECOND VOYAGE

Cartier returned to France with the Iroquois boys and the first corn seen in Europe. He told King Francis I of a possible **Northwest Passage** west of Newfoundland. The explorer also shared the stories of wealthy nations that were reported to be along the route. The king immediately granted Cartier a second voyage.

Cartier set sail from Saint-Malo again on May 19, 1535. His **fleet** included three ships, with 110 men and the two Iroquois boys. After crossing the Atlantic, Cartier sailed through the Strait of Belle Isle again.

On August 10, Cartier's ships reached the northern point of Gaspé **Peninsula**. They entered the bay where they had seen the river on the first voyage. Cartier named the bay and the river St. Lawrence because it was that saint's **feast day**.

One of Cartier's ships was the *Grande Hermine*.

14

King Francis I of France

This time, Cartier sailed his ships up the river. The crew soon reached Donnacona's village, which was called Stadacona. Cartier left the boys in the village with Donnacona and continued exploring upriver. Next, the ships reached Hochelaga, another Native American village. Cartier climbed a mountain at the edge of this village and named it *Mont Réal*, meaning "Mount Royal."

Looking west from the mountain, Cartier could see **rapids** on the St. Lawrence River. He named them *La Chine Rapids*, meaning the "China Rapids." He thought that China lay just beyond them.

By this time, it was winter. So, Cartier decided to turn back. The crew spent the winter at a fort they had built near Stadacona. It was a hard winter. Twenty-five of the crew members died of **scurvy**.

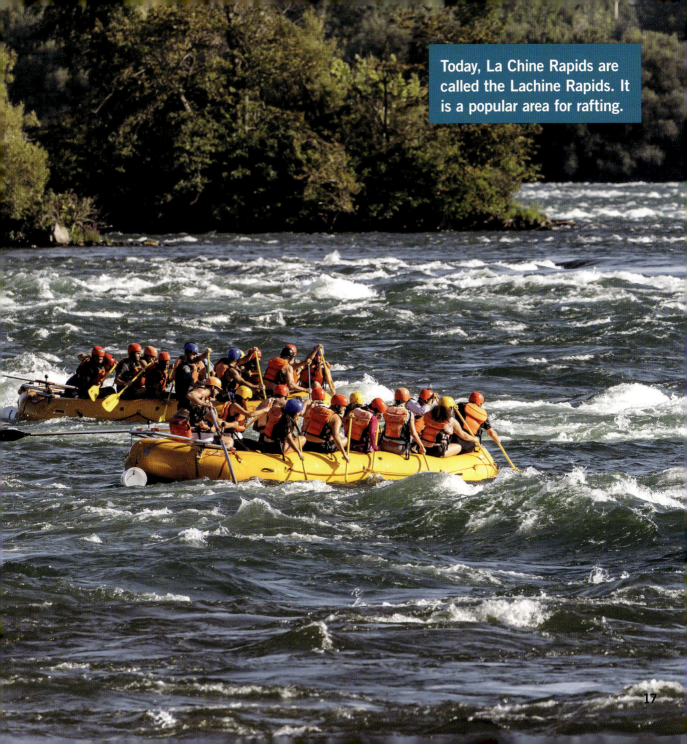

Today, La Chine Rapids are called the Lachine Rapids. It is a popular area for rafting.

During Cartier's stay at the fort, the Iroquois shared tales about a wealthy kingdom to the north. They called it Saguenay, and they said it was full of gold and other treasures. Unfortunately, the Frenchmen didn't understand that these were just stories the Iroquois told for amusement.

Cartier was eager to report to King Francis I about the riches in the stories. When spring arrived, Cartier sailed back to France. Among Cartier's passengers were Donnacona and some other members of the Iroquois. They landed in Saint-Malo on July 16, 1536.

WOULD YOU?

Would you have believed the stories the Iroquois told? Make up your own story about the riches of Canada.

On this second voyage, Cartier had uncovered the St. Lawrence River as an entry point to an unknown continent. He still hoped this continent would provide a passage to China.

The St. Lawrence River today

THIRD VOYAGE

Cartier was eager to make a third expedition. He wanted to search for Saguenay and the riches the Iroquois had talked about. Chief Donnacona fueled the excitement.

Once Donnacona realized how much the Europeans prized gold and jewels, he **embellished** his stories. He swore there were many riches in Canada and Saguenay. Cartier wanted to look for these riches. However, a war between France and Spain **postponed** the voyage for five years.

The third journey was much different from Cartier's earlier voyages. The expedition included several ships and several hundred people, including farmers and convicts. This voyage was for more than exploring. The French aimed to **colonize** the area.

For this reason, the king assigned Jean-François de La Rocque de Roberval to command the expedition. The nobleman was named lieutenant general of the North American territory. Roberval took a long time to prepare for the voyage. He had to organize an army and supplies for the colony.

Jean-François de La Rocque de Roberval

Cartier was in command of just five ships. He was ready before Roberval. So, Cartier left the port of Saint-Malo on May 23, 1541, without the lieutenant general. Cartier waited several weeks at Newfoundland for Roberval. When he did not arrive, Cartier sailed up the St. Lawrence River to Stadacona.

Cartier searched for a good site for the colony. He chose a point near the Cap Rouge River, west of the village. This site had good land for farming and trees for fuel and building. The settlers built a fort called Cap Rouge and prepared for winter.

A map of the St. Lawrence River from Cartier's time

Meanwhile, Cartier and his crew looked for the promised treasures. They were excited to find gold and diamonds! They explored the St. Lawrence River until it was no longer **navigable** by his ships. But Cartier didn't find Saguenay. Cartier and his crew sailed back to the fort for the winter.

The following months were difficult. The Native Americans were hostile when they realized the French intended to stay. Many of the French were sick with **scurvy**. In addition, Roberval had not arrived with supplies for the colony.

Roberval still had not arrived by the spring. So, Cartier started his return voyage to France. He met Roberval in Newfoundland. Roberval ordered Cartier to return to the settlement, but Cartier refused. He continued to France with his treasure. However, back in Saint-Malo, Cartier learned that the diamonds and gold were really quartz and pyrite. The treasure was nearly worthless!

WOULD YOU?

Would you disobey Roberval's order and return to France? What do you think were Cartier's reasons for returning to France?

In the 1500s, quartz wasn't useful. But today it is used in jewelry, ceramics, and glass.

Pyrite is an iron mineral. But it looks a lot like gold. So, pyrite is often called fool's gold.

CARTIER'S LEGACY

Cartier spent the rest of his life near Saint-Malo. He died on September 1, 1557. Cartier did not find the riches he sought. He didn't uncover the **Northwest Passage**. And his attempt to **colonize** Canada failed.

However, Cartier accomplished many great things. He explored waterways and lands unknown to Europeans. He also sailed farther into the New World than explorers had before him.

Cartier's documentation of his expeditions was the best of his time. Fifty years after his death, the explorer's detailed notes helped the French successfully colonize Canada. For nearly 150 years, Canada was known as New France.

The British took over Canada in 1759. But this change in power did not end the French influence that Jacques Cartier had established. French traditions and **culture** continue there to this day.

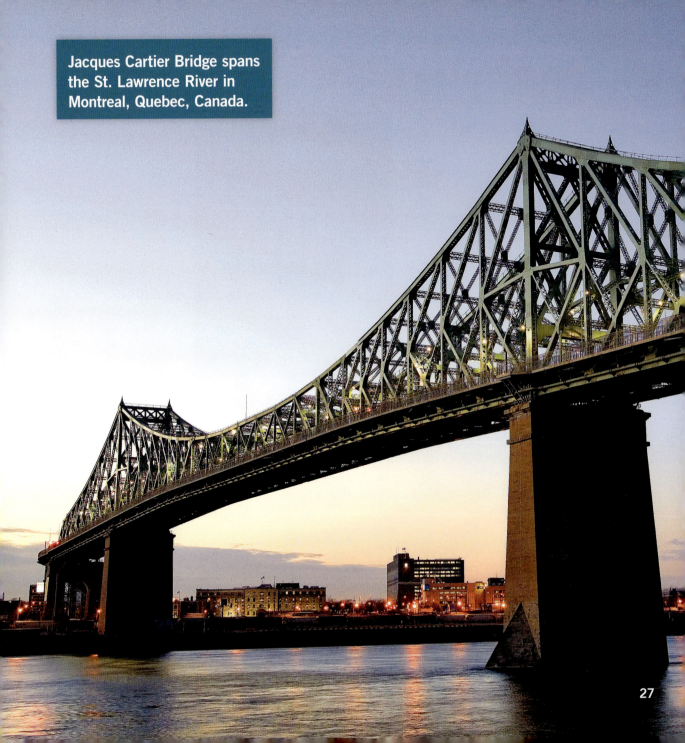
Jacques Cartier Bridge spans the St. Lawrence River in Montreal, Quebec, Canada.

TIMELINE

1534
Cartier makes his first voyage to North America. He claims land for France.

1491
Jacques Cartier is born in Saint-Malo, France.

1520
Cartier marries Catherine des Granches.

1535
Cartier makes his second voyage to North America. He explores the St. Lawrence River.

1541
Cartier makes his third voyage to North America. He tries to start a French colony.

1557
Cartier dies on September 1 near Saint-Malo.

GLOSSARY

colonize—to establish a colony.

culture—the customs, arts, and tools of a nation or a people at a certain time.

embellish—to make something more attractive by adding details that may not be true.

feast day—a religious ceremony and feast to celebrate a saint.

fleet—a group of ships under one command.

indigenous—living, existing, or produced originally in a particular region or environment.

interpreter—a person who translates the words that someone is speaking into a different language.

navigable—deep and wide enough for boats and ships to travel on or through.

Northwest Passage—a supposed sea passage along the north coast of North America. It would connect the Pacific and Atlantic oceans.

peninsula—land that sticks out into water.

postpone—to put off until a later time.

rapids—a fast-moving part of a river. Rocks or logs often break the surface of the water in this area.

scurvy—a disease caused by a lack of vitamin C.

30

SAYING IT

Dieppe—DYEHP

Gaspé Peninsula—ga-SPAY puh-NIHNT-suh-luh

Hochelaga—hah-shuh-LA-guh

Jacques Cartier—zhahk kar-tyay

Jean-François de La Rocque de Roberval—zhahn-frahn-swah duh la rawk duh raw-behr-val

Labrador—LA-bruh-dawr

Magdalen Islands—MAG-duh-luhn EYE-luhnds

Saguenay—sa-guh-NAY

ONLINE RESOURCES

To learn more about Jacques Cartier, please visit **abdobooklinks.com** or scan this QR code. These links are routinely monitored and updated to provide the most current information available.

31

INDEX

Asia, 4, 8, 16, 18
Atlantic Ocean, 4, 6, 14

birth, 6
Brazil, 6

Canada, 4, 6, 8, 10, 14, 16, 20, 22, 24, 26
childhood, 6
China, 4, 16, 18
colonization, 20, 22, 24, 26

death, 26
Donnacona, 10, 16, 18, 20

education, 6
England, 26
Europe, 4, 6, 14, 20, 26

family, 6
France, 4, 6, 8, 10, 14, 18, 20, 22, 24, 26
Francis I (king of France), 8, 14, 18

Iroquois, 10, 14, 18, 20

Mi'kmaq, 8

Native Americans, 8, 10, 14, 16, 18, 20, 24
New World, 26
North America, 6, 20
North Carolina, 6
Northwest Passage, 4, 14, 26

Roberval, Jean-François de La Rocque de, 20, 22, 24

Spain, 20
St. Lawrence River, 4, 10, 14, 16, 18, 22, 24

trading, 8
treasure, 4, 8, 10, 18, 20, 24, 26

Verrazano, Giovanni da, 6